T0210399

The ABRSM
SINGING FOR
MUSICAL THEATRE
Songbook
Grade 5

LIST A	**No One Is Alone** Into the Woods	3
	China Doll Marguerite	8
	No Other Love Me and Juliet	12
	Leaning on a Lamp Post Me and My Girl	17
LIST B	**It Takes Two** Hairspray	21
	Night Will Come Groundhog Day the Musical	26
	What's Wrong With Me? Mean Girls	32
	Just Around the Riverbend Pocahontas	37
LIST C	**Backwoods Barbie** 9 to 5 The Musical	43
	You're Welcome Moana	49
	Honey Bun South Pacific	57
	The Kite (Charlie Brown's Kite) You're a Good Man, Charlie Brown	62

This is a selection of the songs from the ABRSM Singing for Musical Theatre syllabus. For the complete repertoire lists and full details of exam requirements, please see the current syllabus at www.abrsm.org/sfmt. Musical theatre is a vibrant and energetic contemporary art form, and with songs exploring different characters and styles of music there should be something for everyone, whether you are preparing for an exam, audition, or the stage, or just because you love singing songs from shows!

ABRSM would like to thank Rachel Lyske for her invaluable advice.

First published in 2020 by Hal Leonard Europe Limited and ABRSM (Publishing) Ltd, a wholly owned subsidiary of ABRSM.

Exclusively distributed worldwide by Hal Leonard Europe Limited

ISBN 978 1 83992 005 9
AB 3998

Music Origination by John Rogers — Top Score Music
Printed on materials from sustainable sources

ABRSM

World headquarters, contact:
Hal Leonard
7777 West Bluemound Road
Milwaukee, WI 53213 Email:
info@halleonard.com

In Europe, contact:
Hal Leonard Europe Limited
1 Red Place
London, W1K 6PL
Email: info@halleonardeurope.com

In Australia, contact:
Hal Leonard Australia Pty. Ltd.
4 Lentara Court
Cheltenham, Victoria, 3192 Australia
Email: info@halleonard.com.au

NO ONE IS ALONE

Into the Woods

Words and music by
Stephen Sondheim (born 1930)

The song is an ensemble number in the show. This is the composer's official version for solo voice and piano.

CHINA DOLL

Marguerite

Music by Michel Legrand (1932-2019)
Lyrics by Alain Boublil (born 1941)
Herbert Kretzmer (born 1925)
Adapted from original French lyrics by Alain Boublil

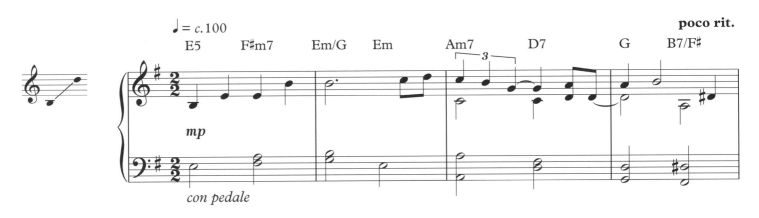

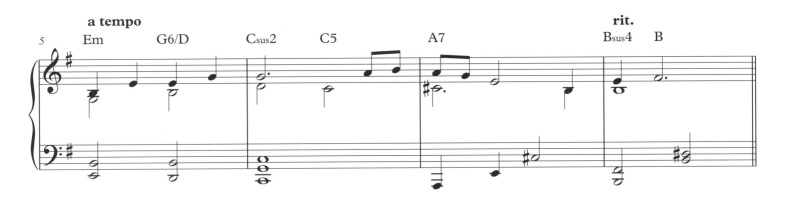

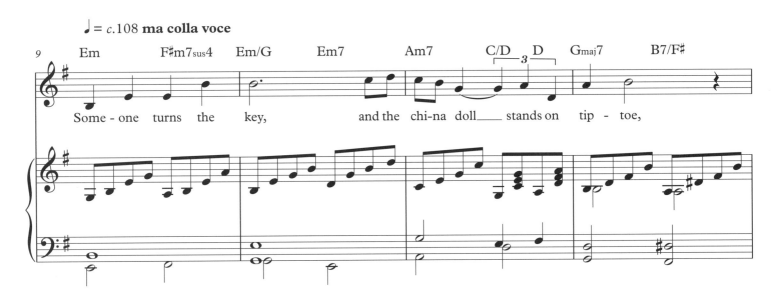

NO OTHER LOVE

Me and Juliet

Lyrics by Oscar Hammerstein II (1895–1960)
Music by Richard Rodgers (1902–79)

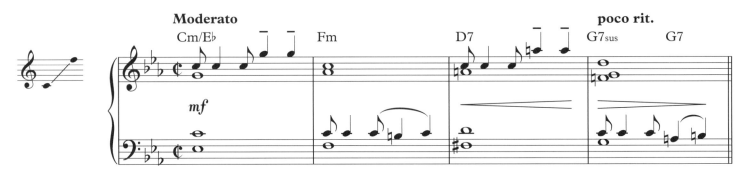

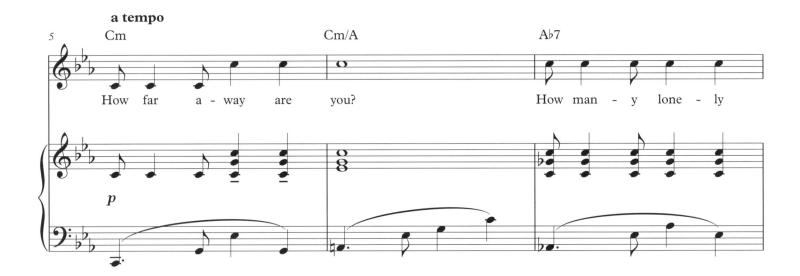

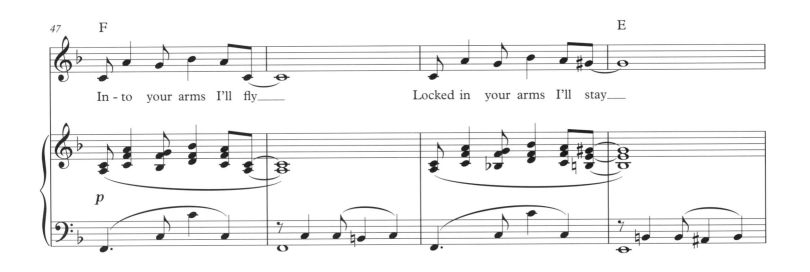

In - to your arms I'll fly___ Locked in your arms I'll stay___

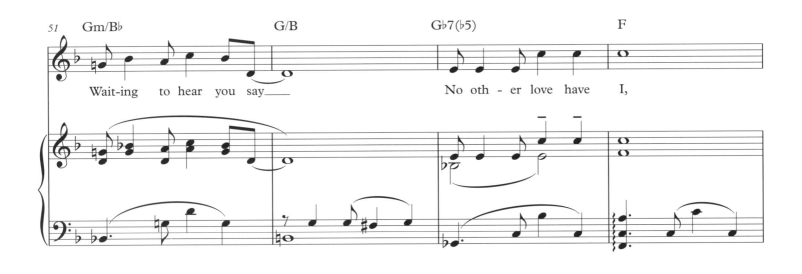

Wait-ing to hear you say___ No oth - er love have I,

No oth - er love.___

LEANING ON A LAMP POST

Me and My Girl

Words and music by
Noel Gay (1898-1954)

Lean - ing on a lamp, may-be you think I look a tramp, or you may think I'm hang - ing round to steal a car; _____ But

IT TAKES TWO

Hairspray

Music by Marc Shaiman (born 1959)
Lyrics by Marc Shaiman (born 1959)
Scott Wittman (born 1954)

'60s rhythm ballad

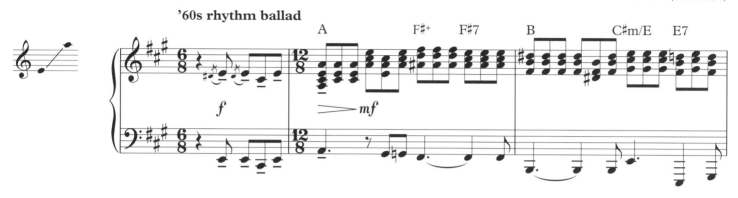

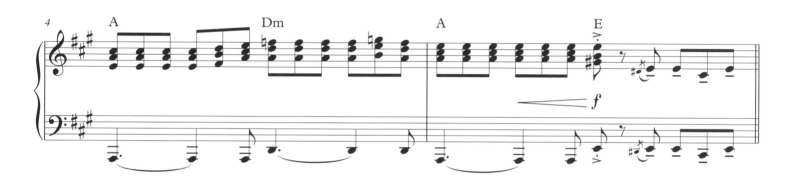

They say it's a man's world. Well, that can - not_____ be de - nied.
A king ain't a king with - out the pow'r be - hind the throne._____
Just like Frank - ie Av - a - lon_____ has his fav - 'rite_____ Mouse - ke - teer,

Exam requirements: without first repeat

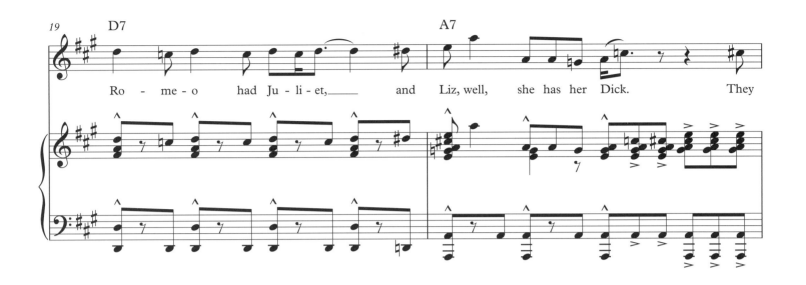

Ro - me - o had Ju - li - et,_____ and Liz, well, she has her Dick. They

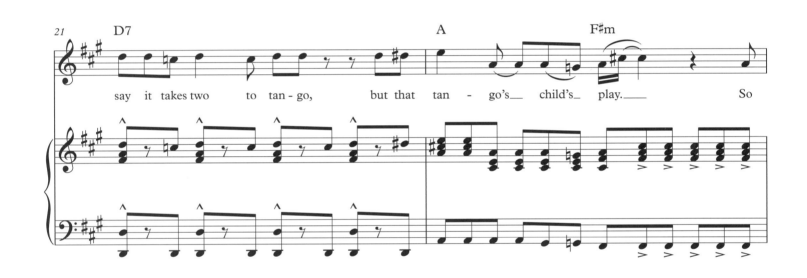

say it takes two to tan - go, but that tan - go's___ child's___ play.___ So

D.S. al Coda

take me to the dance floor,_ and we'll twist the night a - way.___

CODA

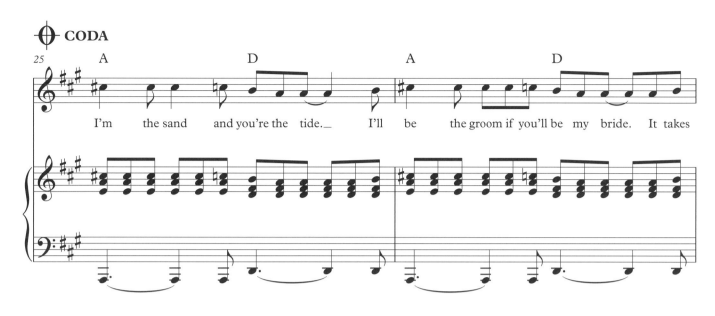

I'm the sand and you're the tide.— I'll be the groom if you'll be my bride. It takes

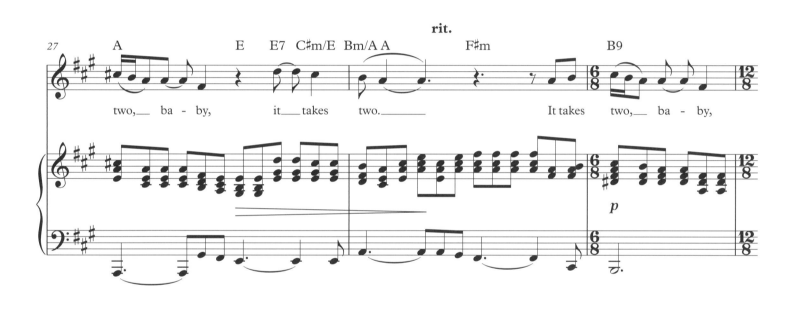

two,— ba - by, it takes two.— It takes two, baby,

rit.

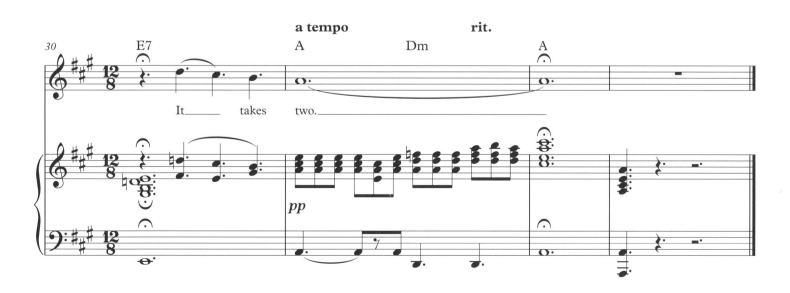

a tempo   rit.

It takes two.

NIGHT WILL COME

Groundhog Day the Musical

Words and music by
Tim Minchin (born 1975)

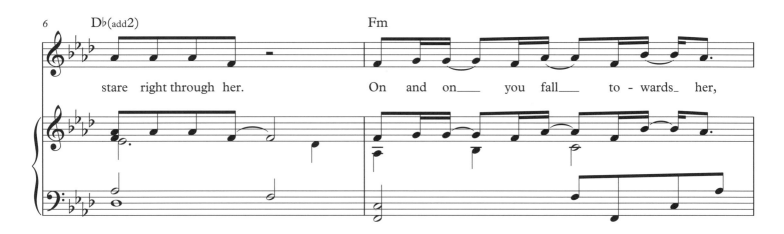

Exam requirements: any two verses

WHAT'S WRONG WITH ME?

Mean Girls

Words by Nell Benjamin
Music by Jeff Richmond (born 1961)

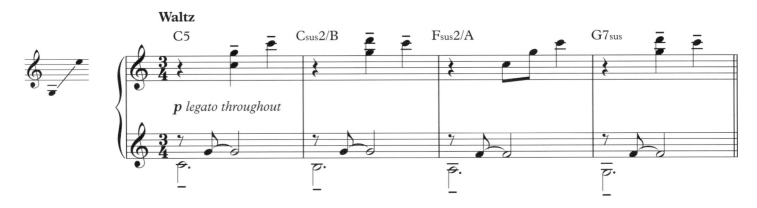

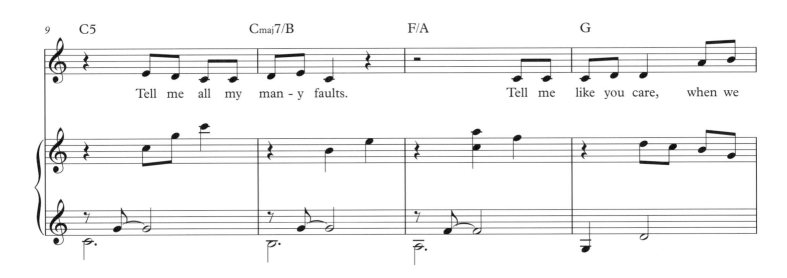

JUST AROUND THE RIVERBEND

Pocahontas

Music by Alan Menken (born 1949)
Lyrics by Stephen Schwartz (born 1948)

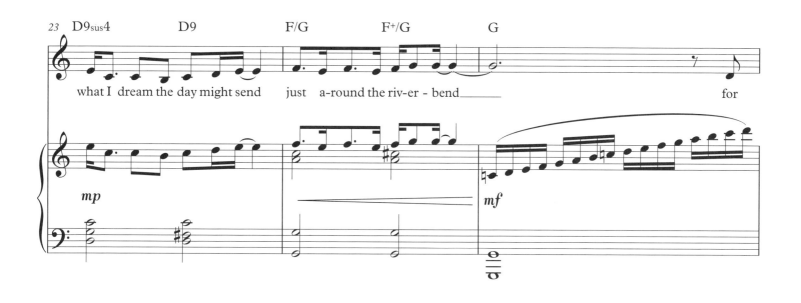

what I dream the day might send just a-round the riv-er - bend_____ for

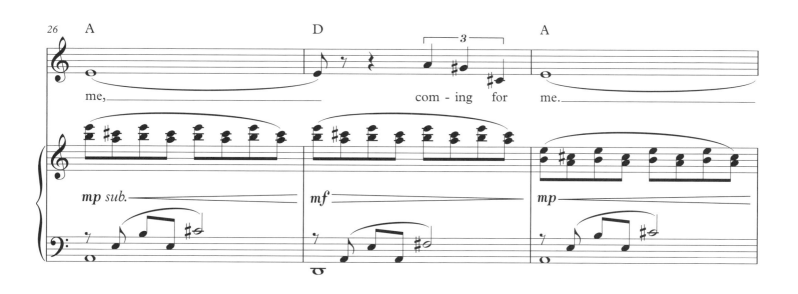

me,_____ com - ing for me._____

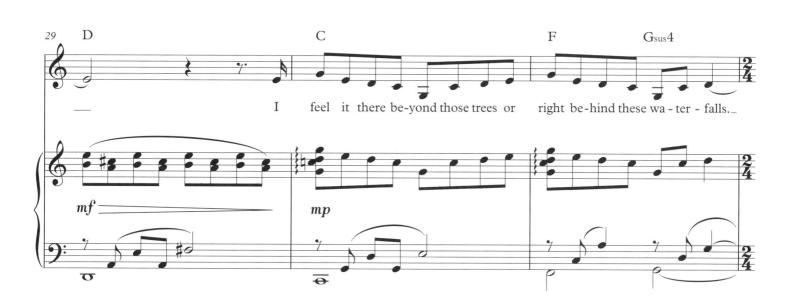

__ I feel it there be-yond those trees or right be-hind these wa - ter - falls._

40

AB 3998

just a-round the riv-er - bend be-yond the shore, some-where past the sea. Don't

know what for... why do all my dreams ex-tend just a-round the riv-er - bend?

Just a - round the riv - er - bend.

BACKWOODS BARBIE

9 to 5 The Musical

Words and music by
Dolly Parton (born 1946)

Moderate country feel

am.__ The way I look_ is just a coun-try_ girl's i - dea_ of

glam. I

grew up poor_ and rag-ged, just a sim-ple coun-try girl. I

want-ed to_ be pret-ty more than an-y-thing in the world,

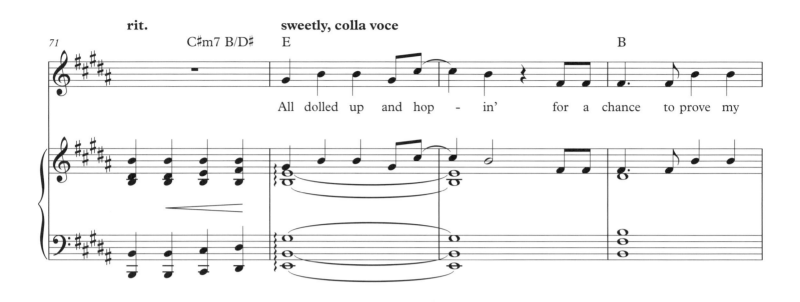

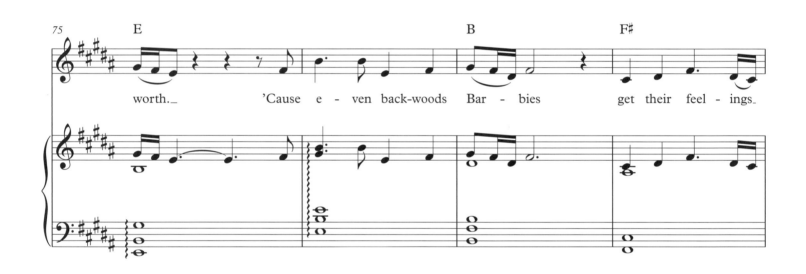

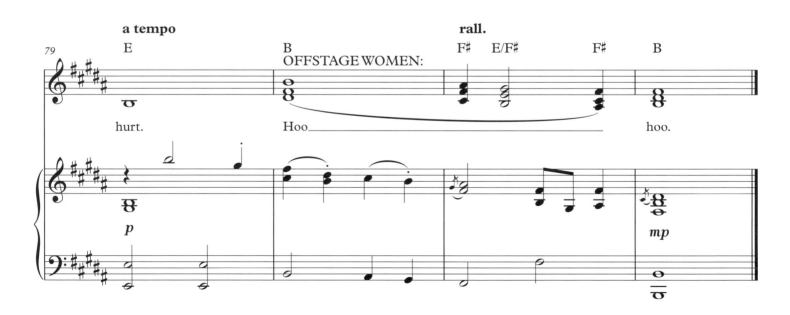

YOU'RE WELCOME

Moana

Music and lyrics by
Lin-Manuel Miranda (born 1980)

Exam requirements: rap optional; singing upper line on pp. 52–54

it's o - kay:__ you're wel - come.
(You're wel - come.)
Well, come to think of it, I got - ta go.
(Ha, ha, ha.)

Hey, it's your day__ to say,__ 'You're wel - come,' 'cause
(Hey, hey, hey, hey!) (You're wel - come.)

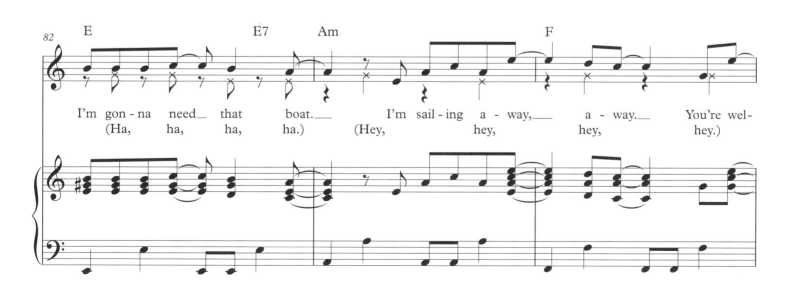

I'm gon - na need__ that boat.__ I'm sail - ing a - way,__ a - way.__ You're wel-
(Ha, ha, ha, ha.) (Hey, hey, hey, hey.)

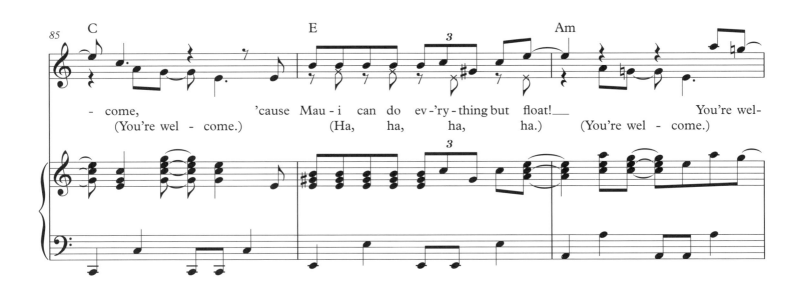

Additional Lyrics

Rap: Kid, honestly, I could go on and on.
I could explain ev'ry nat'ral phenomenon.
The tide? The grass? The ground?
Oh, that was Maui, just messing around.

I killed an eel, I buried its guts,
Sprouted a tree: now you got coconuts!
What's the lesson? What is the takeaway?
Don't mess with Maui when he's on a breakaway.

And the tapestry here in my skin
Is a map of the vict'ries I win!
Look where I've been! I make ev'rything happen!
Look at that mean mini Maui, just tickety
Tappin'! Heh, heh, heh,
Heh, heh, heh, hey!

HONEY BUN

South Pacific

Lyrics by Oscar Hammerstein II (1895-1960)
Music by Richard Rodgers (1902-79)

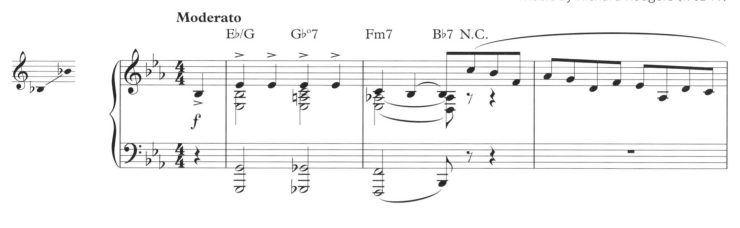

Exam requirements: without repeat

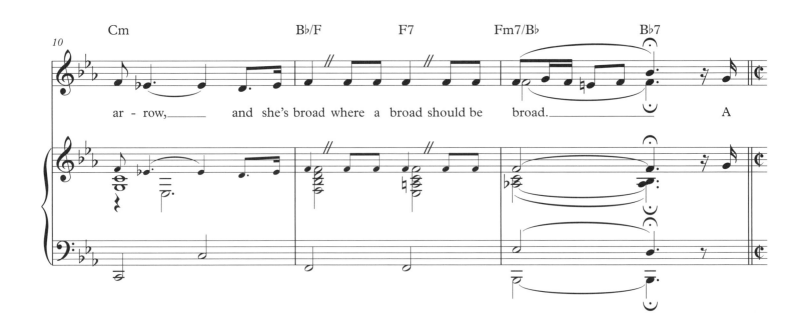

Refrain, lively

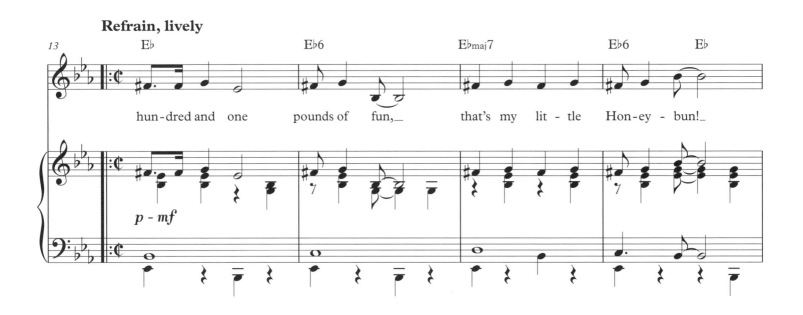

cook - ie who can cook you till__ you're done, (Ain't be - in' fun - ny.)

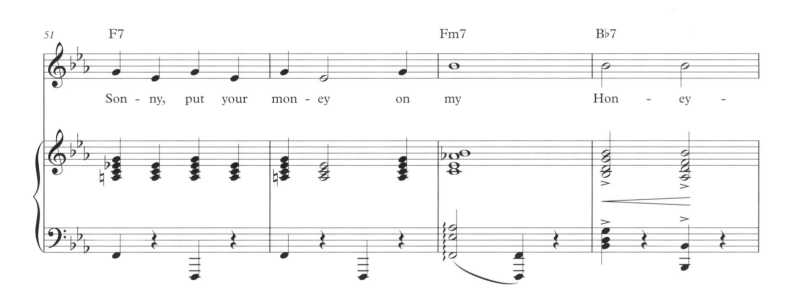

Son - ny, put your mon - ey on my Hon - ey -

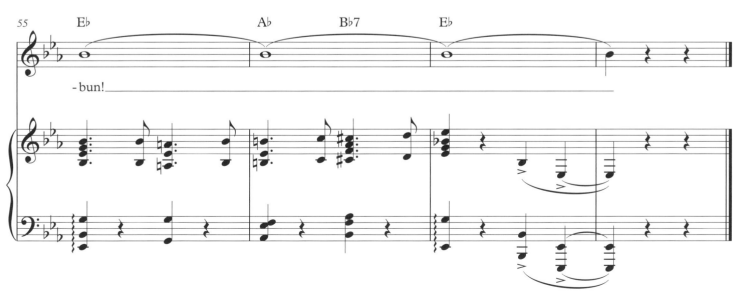

-bun!

THE KITE
(CHARLIE BROWN'S KITE)

You're a Good Man, Charlie Brown

Words and music by
Clark Gesner (1938-2002)

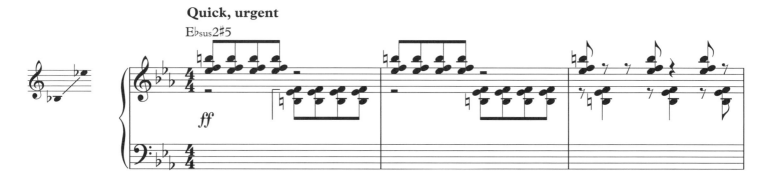

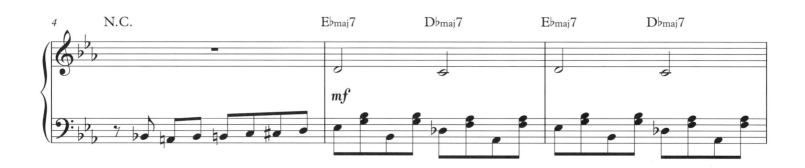

CHARLIE BROWN:

Lit - tle more speed, lit - tle more rope, Lit - tle more wind, lit - tle more hope.